DINNER WITH
D. W. GRIFFITH

AND OTHER MEMORIES

DINNER WITH D. W. GRIFFITH

AND OTHER MEMORIES

JOSEPH WOODSON OGLESBY

BORGO PRESS

Set in Sabon

Edited by Kathleen Martin

BORGO PRESS is an imprint of Wildside Press
PO Box 301, Holicong, PA 18928-0301
www.wildsidepress.com

For more information contact Wildside Press

ISBN 0-8095-5071-7 (hc)
ISBN 0-8095-5072-5 (tpb)

The author at age seven in his aviator's cap.

To Marianna Oglesby and Shane Woodson,
who believed in the magic of my words
even when I didn't.

Table of Contents

The Night Caller.....9

Tiger in the Alley.....17

The Old Men in Black Suits.....21

The Tin Boy.....25

Dinner with D. W. Griffith.....33

The Piano Player.....45

The Great Flood.....51

The Belated Christmas Gift.....67

A Taste of the Country.....71

Black Market Spy.....77

The Murder Suspect.....85

A Ride in the Paddy Wagon.....93

"Buttons".....97

The Two Faces of Love.....101

The Death Sentence.....105

Joe's Place.....111

Afterword: An Ode and Thanks.....117

The Night Caller

When I was growing up in Louisville in the 1930s, it was a slow, lazy, dreamy city, more Southern than Northern, its many parts connected by orange streetcars that crackled and cast bright sparks into the air as they sped along their electric lines. The tawny Ohio River marked the city's northern and western borders and marshland and green hills its southern extremity, while the east end, rising high above the valley, gazed affectionately toward the fabled Bluegrass some fifty miles distant.

Antique fences decorated with iron tulips and roses and fleurs-de-lis defended the privacy of the Italianate, Renaissance Revival and Neo-Greco mansions on Third Street, some of which had been converted into apartment buildings. My mother and father and I and my puppy, Lorenzo, lived in the second-floor apartment of one of these converted Italianate mansions. Its windows were tall, and a beautiful blue mosaic tile covered the vestibule floor.

The rooms in our apartment branched off a long hall, connected to the ground floor by front and rear staircases of dark wood. The transom above the parlor was a long rectangle of glass that could be lowered on summer days to cool the apartment. I can see my mother now, in a long taffeta dress with lace collar, opening the transom for a breeze and drawing shut the heavy draperies at the tall windows against the heat before reclining on her fainting couch for an afternoon nap.

In the apartment below us lived Mrs. Stone, a large woman who communicated with the dead. Her cheeks were orange with rouge and her lips scarlet. On her fat fingers she wore silver rings and around her curly red hair a bright scarf.

Her husband, a small man with liver marks on his frail hands, operated a tool-sharpening business in a large wooden shed behind the house. An Orange Crush decal held together a cracked pane in his shop's door. Through one of the clear, unbroken panes, I used to watch him work, splinters of light shooting from the tongue of a sickle or the blade of a butcher knife as he pressed it against the grindstone. He wore a faint smile as he worked, as if pleased with what he did. I hardly ever saw him in the main house and never once in Mrs. Stone's parlor, where she conducted her own business.

Her parlor, larger and cooler and better appointed than ours, was carpeted with a huge red oriental rug. A Victorian couch stood before the front windows. On the ornate white marble mantel rested two long silver horns. In the middle of the room stood a huge library table with chairs arranged around it. At night two Tiffany lamps illuminated the room in a soft, lemony glow.

In this room Mrs. Stone called forth the dead. Their voices came to her from the mouths of the silver horns. Seated at the head of the long library table—her hands linked to those of the person on each side of her, and those persons' hands in turn linked to others, forming a chain— she conducted her séances.

From the upstairs windows, my mother and I used to

watch Mrs. Stone's guests arrive. One old lady, who wore lavender dresses, came to the séances in a chauffeur-driven black Packard. The regulars also included two sisters, small women with snow-white hair who arrived by cab. Mother told me the sisters were trying to reach their papa on the other side. They wanted to find out where he'd stashed his money, since they were nearly penniless, and neither of them was trained to do anything to make a living. But I never really believed Mrs. Stone talked with the dead. Or that the dead could talk. I thought Mrs. Stone played Halloween games the year around.

My doubts about the powers of the dead vanished one summer night. A steady rain had fallen most of the day and into the night until the asphalt streets were shiny black. Passing cars splashed rainwater onto the sidewalks long after the rain stopped. The rain brought out the scent of the honeysuckle along the iron fence out front and the roses in the side garden.

Mrs. Stone and my mother were taking the night air and talking on the front porch. Mrs. Stone was complaining that her husband, Malachai, hadn't taken her to the latest Claudette Colbert movie as they'd planned; instead, he was working late in his shop. As they talked, I watched night traffic from my perch on the balustrade. I was fascinated by the gleaming yellow ribbons created on the mirror-like street by the lights of the passing cars.

Suddenly, we heard a loud rapping inside the house.

"What is that?" my mother asked in an uneasy voice.

"Perhaps Malachai locked himself out of the apartment," Mrs. Stone said. "I'll go see." She started quickly toward the front door.

"I think I'll go in with you, Rose," my mother said. "It's time for bed, anyway. Come along, Joe."

"It's too early for bed," I whined.

"Hush," my mother said.

Through the leaded glass of the front door, my mother and Mrs. Stone glimpsed a luminous figure in the dimly lit hall—a woman dressed in white. As we entered the vestibule, the woman retreated.

"Please don't run from us," Mrs. Stone said, used to dealing with ghosts. "We want to help you, dear."

But, without ever turning toward us, the apparition moved swiftly and gracefully away from us into the far regions of the hall and up the dark rear staircase. Mrs. Stone rushed after her, while my mother and I, shaken by what we'd seen, held hands, anxiously awaiting the medium's return.

Time passed slowly. The summer rain started again, pecking at the front door like angry crows.

At last Mrs. Stone returned, pale and edgy.

"I lost her," she said flatly.

"Who was she?" my mother asked.

"I never saw her face," Mrs. Stone said, "but she seemed familiar."

"I don't understand," Mother said. "Apparently she wanted to gain our attention, but she fled when we responded to her rapping."

"The ways of the dead are inscrutable," Mrs. Stone said. Her face darkened. "But I venture we will understand this visitation before the night ends."

When we reached our apartment, my mother asked my father if a lady in white had knocked on our door.

"Why, no," he said, putting down the evening newspaper. "Were you expecting company?"

"No, of course not."

Used to Mother's sometimes peculiar ways, he returned to his newspaper.

We'd been in bed perhaps an hour when a soft knock sounded on our door. In her rose silk kimono, my mother rushed to answer it. It was Mrs. Stone.

"I just received a phone call from Sarasota," she said. "My sister, Elizabeth, died in a car accident about ten o'clock tonight."

My mother gasped. "That was about the time we saw the woman in white."

"Yes," Mrs. Stone said. "It was Elizabeth. She came to say goodbye."

Mrs. Stone conducted séances in her parlor.

My dog Lorenzo and I in Mrs. Stone's parlor, circa 1935.

Tiger in the Alley

Nearly every summer night I used to go with my daddy to Corso's, a neighborhood bar. We usually got there through an alley because it was shorter that way.

In one particularly dark stretch of the alley, several large acacia trees, which we called stink trees, rose past the line of an old board fence. The dilapidated frame house behind the fence was abandoned and its windows broken; its shutters rattled eerily when a high wind blew. The stink trees were so large and exotic, they seemed like jungle trees to me. One night I asked my daddy if jungle trees looked like stink trees. He said he believed they did.

The next time we came up the alley, I was walking ahead of my daddy. I was imagining myself an explorer in Africa. Suddenly something moved behind the high board fence where the stink trees grew. I stopped, turning around to be sure Daddy was there. The alley was pitch black.

"Did you hear something, Daddy?" I asked.

"Uh-huh," he said. "Sounded like a tiger to me."

"A tiger!"

"Let's go see," he said.

"But he might jump the fence and eat us up."

"Not as long as I'm here," Daddy said.

His huge hand swallowed mine as we stepped cautiously to the fence. Again something moved behind it. I felt goose bumps pop out on my arms. I was sure the tiger was getting ready to leap over the fence. My daddy pressed his face to a crack in the fence, and so did I. The odor of the stink trees swam into my nostrils. I could make out a lot of dark shapes in the grass, but I didn't see any tiger.

"He must've run off," my daddy said. "We scared him."

"Do you really think we scared that old tiger?" I asked.

"Sure we did."

The neon beer sign in Corso's front window beckoned as we left the alley and crossed Fifth Street. Corso's was a men's bar—in those days all bars were men's bars—with plates of free pretzels on the bar top. On weekends the owner, Ed Corso, who liked to juggle a fat cigar in his mouth as he talked, put out slices of ham and cheese, too. For a ten-cent beer, a man could get a free meal.

The bar had its regular customers. They all knew each other and treated each other like family. That meant there were plenty of quarrels and occasionally a fistfight.

My dad was the bar's champion Indian wrestler. My mother never knew this and would have fainted away if she had. She thought Daddy played pool every night at some nice "billiards parlor" and let me go along because I wasn't yet in school.

That night a truck driver challenged my daddy to an Indian wrestling match. Someone cleared a table and set two chairs at it across from each other. Daddy finished his beer and sat down at the table, appraising his opponent for a moment before slamming his elbow onto the table's top and scissoring open his huge right hand. Once the men's hands closed in a vise, the match began. The object was to force the opponent's hand flat onto the table. The game required a lot of arm muscle and considerable lasting power.

My daddy and the trucker were well-matched. As a crowd gathered around, encouraging one or the other, the two wrestlers groaned, their faces firing up like the belly of a potbellied stove in the middle of winter. Their strong arms quivered in an arc across the table.

I saw my daddy's arm start to sink toward the tabletop. I couldn't believe it. No one had ever beaten him. Daddy's eyes closed, as if he were gathering strength from a secret place or saying a prayer. Slowly his arm rose, and I saw the surprise in the truck driver's face. Sweat dampened his forehead as he tried to force my daddy's arm back down. The room had become quiet. Ed stopped mopping the bar top.

Daddy's arm muscle became a thick, straining rope. In one long, sustained drive he forced the trucker's hand onto the table. Everybody cheered, and Ed Corso bought drinks for the house. My daddy was my hero—champion Indian wrestler and tiger-tamer.

The next time we took the alley to Corso's, I was hoping the tiger would be there again. I was walking fast, way ahead of my daddy. Just as I reached the high fence with the jungle trees behind it, I turned. I was going to tell Daddy to hurry up—the tiger might be behind the fence!

Daddy was winding up like a baseball pitcher. He puzzled me for a moment, but then I saw the rock in his hand. I quickly turned my head before he saw me watching him.

The thud came.

"That tiger's back!" Daddy shouted. "Come on, let's watch him through the fence."

I scrambled to the fence and peered into the darkness.

"Can you see him, Joe?" he asked.

"I think I do. His eyes are orange! He has a face like a big pussycat."

That was the first time I ever lied to my daddy.

*My father in his wedding suit, given him
by D.W. Griffith.*

The Old Men in Black Suits

When his grandmother hadn't any chores for him to do, Kenny would come to my house and we'd play together. One of our favorite pastimes, after we tired of playing marbles or racing our scooters up and down the sidewalk, was to sit on the balustrade of my house and watch the people pass.

Kenny was a year older than I, and he had more freedom—sometimes going all the way downtown by himself—so he was wiser to the ways of the world. But the old men in black suits puzzled even him. These old men wore black hats with silky bands and beards that went to a spear point beneath their chins. Kenny knew where they lived—in a gloomy, shuttered brick house on Second Street—but he didn't know what they did inside the house.

One afternoon we spotted one of the bearded men coming up the sidewalk. He had something strung over his shoulder—what appeared to be a sack. We ducked behind the balustrade to watch him without his seeing us. As he came nearer, we saw that whatever the sack held was moving. Something *alive* was inside the burlap, and it was trying frantically to get loose.

"He's got a kid in that sack!" Kenny said. "The old guys are kidnappers."

"We'd better go to the police," I said, staring wide-eyed at Kenny.

He was braver than I. "Nah ... come on, let's follow him."

My legs were trembling and my hands were clammy. I wished Mother would show up and say it was time for supper, or tell Kenny to run along home as she sometimes did. I think she figured him to be a bad influence on me ever since the day she'd caught him showing me how to puff on an Indian cigar, the long, panatela-shaped fruit of a catalpa tree that we dried out on a garage roof. But Mother wasn't anywhere in sight.

"Come on, sissy," Kenny shouted, running off the porch. "He's already turning the corner."

I lagged behind Kenny, figuring that if the old man turned on us and decided maybe he'd put one of us in that big sack, he'd grab Kenny first.

We rounded the corner. The old man was still in sight.

An ice-cream vendor on a bicycle pedaled past, ringing his handlebar bell. I made one last, desperate stab at stopping Kenny. I had a nickel in my knickers. I'd been saving it for three weeks to buy a lead soldier—a machine gunner.

"Hey, let's get a Popsicle. I'll split a grape with you!" I shouted.

"Not now!" Kenny said, looking back at me hatefully. "Hurry up!"

There was no way out for me, I thought. I'd have to go through with it. I gritted my teeth. Even on a moonless night, I wasn't afraid of the pitch-black alley behind our house, and I wasn't afraid of caterpillars or having my mother clean a scraped knee with rubbing alcohol, but I was deathly afraid of those old men in black suits. Seeing that old man with something alive in his sack only confirmed my fears.

We ducked behind the dark, corrugated trunk of a huge tulip poplar tree and watched the old man disappear into the shuttered house.

"Let's go home now," I said.

"No," Kenny said. "Let's go up to the house and see if we can look inside."

We darted across busy Second Street and approached the shuttered house from the lawn of the house next door. The old brick house gave off a dank odor. As we came nearer, we saw a light shining in the basement.

"He's down there!" Kenny said.

We knelt before the dusty rectangular window that looked into the basement. I gasped. Kenny's face turned white. Inside, the old man we'd followed was holding a tin pitcher beneath the corpse of a chicken, hanging upside down from a clothesline. From the chicken's headless body, a stream of bright red blood ran into the pitcher. On the floor lay the burlap sack.

"What's he doing?" I asked.

"He's crazy!" Kenny said, his voice shaking. "The old man's crazy."

"Let's get out of here!" I said.

We started to run off but froze in terror instead as a pair of yellow eyes stared down at us from a towering, bearded face. "Abraham is our cook," the old man said softly. "He is preparing the fowl for our evening meal. It is the belief of our religious order that any fowl we consume must be completely drained of its blood."

I don't think Kenny or I understood exactly what he was saying right then. We were too scared. But the man was friendly, and he was not very old; the beard only made him seem older. He reached into his coat pocket and brought out several pieces of horehound candy. Smiling, he gave us the candy, then walked on around the house.

We meandered back home, discussing all that had happened.

"They're going to eat that old chicken," Kenny said, "claws and all. He cut off the head, but he didn't cut off the chicken's claws or pluck the feathers."

"No, they aren't," I said. "They're going to use the chicken blood in some secret ceremony. Why do you think that other one was so friendly, giving us that candy? He didn't want us telling on them."

"Ah, you have a big imagination, Joey," Kenny said. He always called me *Joey* when he was disgusted with me. He popped a horehound drop into his mouth and made loud sucking sounds.

I wrapped hot fingers around the horehound drops in my knickers pocket. I was going to bury them. I was certain they were poison.

The Tin Boy

$\mathcal{I}$ looked out the window of my first-grade classroom and saw a robin jumping about on a tree branch and wondered why *I* had to stay cooped up in a hot room when the robin could do what he wanted.

I didn't like the peculiar odor of the classroom—a combination of steam heat, chalk and floor wax. I already knew how to read comic books, so I didn't see much point in learning the alphabet. It was an irksome chore for me to do the penmanship lessons, too. Capital *A* and small *a*. Each letter had to be a certain height. The recesses embarrassed me because I didn't know how to skip. The other children skipped as they spun in a circle and sang "Here We Go 'round the Mulberry Bush." I wasn't much of a singer, either.

To relieve my boredom and ineptness, I teased the little girl who sat in front of me. Her name was Alice, and she possessed a beautiful, glossy blond pigtail that she festooned with a different ribbon every day—bright pink or canary yellow or robin's egg blue. I'd yank on her pigtail and she'd turn around with a glower and slap my hand. But she never tattled on me. That February I gave her a Valentine, but I didn't sign it.

The school fire escape was silo-shaped, and it ran from the third to the first floor. After school, we used to pry open the bottom door and shimmy up its spiraling chute. Then we rode down on a burlap sack, sometimes freight-train style—a big boy in front as locomotive, with three or four smaller boys hanging on behind as box cars. I was the coal car. Perry Wilson, because he was the smallest, was usually the caboose. That was the only thing I ever liked about school.

Perry was my best friend at school. My summer friend, Kenny, went to a Catholic school, so I didn't see him as often. Perry filled the gap. He was small but tough. He always wore a sheep-lined coat to school, even in warm weather. His eyes were an icy blue and his hair blond and curly. He looked like a little lamb. The crescents of his fingernails were especially large and very pale white. Perry was an orphan and lived at the Louisville Baptist Orphans Home on First Street, also known as the Home for Helpless Children.

One day the class toughies ganged up on me with their waterguns in the boys' restroom. I didn't have a watergun but I fought back, swinging my fists in every direction. The spurts of cold water stung when they hit me in the eyes. Jets of water ran down my neck past my collar and tickled me.

When Perry came in, he knew just what to do. Dashing to a sink, he turned on the cold-water tap and cupped the running water in his hands, tossing it at my tormentors. This was heavy artillery, and the toughies soon cleared out of the restroom.

Our in-school skirmishes were minor though compared to the after-school fights. In the whole neighborhood there were only two Jewish boys, and they were the other boys' scapegoats. Everyone picked on Hans and Harry. Their only defense was in hanging together.

One Friday afternoon we all lay siege to the pair, holed up in the screened-in back porch of Harry's house. His mama was gone. From an adjoining field we threw rocks and half-bricks at them, daring them to come out. As we moved in closer, our missiles tore holes in the screen. We didn't stop until we heard the police siren.

We were cruel, as many children are when not closely supervised. One day after school I used an older boy's BB gun to shoot a blue jay. I spotted the bird in a pear tree. Taking aim, I squeezed the trigger, but I really couldn't believe it when the bird toppled to the ground, thrashing its wings. A sudden sadness swept through me as I rushed to where the bird lay and picked it up. It was still warm, but the life was ebbing from its body. I stared at the small black hole in its breast where blood oozed out. Even after it had gone stiff, I worked the bird's wings with my hands, thinking I might bring it back to life.

As I dug a small grave near the shed where Mr. Stone's tool-sharpening shop once had been, I thought of watching the yellow sparks fly from his sharpening stone on a velvety black night. That seemed long ago. I raked the earth over the blue jay's body and left a brick as a tombstone.

After that I never killed a living thing. Even caterpillars, which I'd once loved to squash to see the yellow "paint" spurt from them, I left alone. I didn't even catch June bugs anymore and tie a string to them and swirl them around in the air, or imprison lightning bugs in a jar to make a lantern.

Winter came. The skies were pearl gray. Frost caked the windowpanes. My hand would nearly stick to the iron gate when I opened it to enter the school grounds. The halls stank with steam heat and the smell of galoshes and wool linings of coats.

One night it snowed. The next day the snow was ankle deep. My daddy volunteered to walk me to school since it happened to be one of his rare days off during the week. But I was too grown-up now for that. As I walked to school, the icy wind took my breath. I banded my wool scarf around my face as I had seen Gary Cooper do in a desert movie when there was a sandstorm.

At recess that day, Perry showed me a picture of the Tin Man in "The Wizard of Oz" and excitedly told me about him. The Tin Man wanted a heart. I noticed that Perry was particularly pale; the crescents on his nails seemed even larger. He went straight home to the orphanage that day after school.

Snow kept falling. A lot of children didn't make it to school the next day, or the day after, so I didn't think too much about Perry's absence. But on the third day I began to worry. Was he sick? Did some family adopt him?

Late that afternoon I decided to walk over to the orphanage. I had never visited there before. It was an enormous Victorian structure of red brick and sandstone. A high iron fence surrounded the grounds. Tall trees flanked the walkway to the entrance.

I paused near the main gate, thinking I might see Perry throwing snowballs in the yard or looking out one of the windows. But I saw no one. The tall Gothic windows were dark on all three floors of the building. A bitter wind blew whirlpools of snow across the yard. A shaggy dog with its tail tucked ran past me on the sidewalk. The place frightened me. I harbored the fear that, if I entered the grounds of the building, someone might lock me up and make me an orphan, too.

With much trepidation, I approached the wide double doors, paned with leaded glass, and peeked into the huge hall of the orphanage. A sprawling fern in a brass urn sat to the right of the door. Yellow leaves that had fallen from it lay scattered on the red carpeting. A cork bulletin board hung on one wall with various notices tacked to it.

I entered, planning to ask the first person I saw where I could find Perry Wilson. But no one appeared. Wandering about the building, I found myself before an office with an enamel nameplate on it: SUPERINTENDENT. I wasn't sure what that meant, but I had an inkling. I knocked on the door.

A tall, thin lady in an amber velvet dress opened it. Her gray hair was tight in a bun. She was so skinny her veins stood out like blue cords on her hands. Her false teeth made her smile seem strange.

"I'm looking for Perry Wilson," I said.

The lady's smile vanished. "Are you a schoolmate of his?" she asked.

"He's my best friend," I said.

She patted my head. "I'm afraid I have some sad news for you," she said. She hesitated, as if deliberating whether to tell me.

"What is it?" I asked.

"Little Perry was a very sick boy," she said softly. "He had a bad heart, damaged by rheumatic fever. During the night, he passed away. But he's in heaven now, and he's happy."

I ran from the building into the freezing air. I kept running until I was exhausted and the tears on my cheeks were icy. I wouldn't understand until I was much older why Perry had been so interested in the Tin Man.

The Louisville Baptist Orphans Home
at 1022 South First Street.

Perry Wilson, a resident of Louisville Baptist Orphans Home, is seated on the front row, second from right, in this 1939 photo.

Dinner with D. W. Griffith

The road to Grandmother's house was so snaky it crossed the railroad tracks nine times between Louisville and where she lived in La Grange. But the occasional Sunday trips were always worth it, since we ate dinner with her. She was the best cook in Oldham County.

She always served two meats, her standards being roast beef and fried country ham in red-eye gravy. In addition, she offered six or seven vegetables—fresh from the garden in summer—and lemon meringue or apple or cherry pie. She did her cooking in an old-fashioned kitchen with a kerosene stove and iron skillets. All the water she used came from a huge wooden rain barrel that sat just outside her kitchen door.

Trips to her house were more fun in the winter, when the country landscape resembled the Currier & Ives prints on her dining-room walls: skaters in bright mufflers cutting figure eights on a thickly iced farm pond ... a horse-drawn sleigh plowing a crisp path through crusty snow toward a farmhouse in the distance, smoke pluming from its chimney ... weeping willows along creek banks bearing long icicles that glistened in the sun, brighter than tinsel.

Whenever Cousin David (film director David Wark Griffith) returned home to La Grange, he was a regular diner at Grandmother's Sunday dinners. One memorable Sunday, Granddaddy answered the door—something he rarely did—with the news that Cousin David had arrived from New York the day before and was expected anytime. Grandmother had been in the kitchen since dawn preparing his favorite dishes. He especially loved her high-rising biscuits and lemon meringue pie. Glassware and china sparkled on the long dining table. Even Granddaddy had been polished. He wore a black suit and black string tie and had been given specific instructions by my grandmother not to stuff his napkin into his collar but to lay it across his lap.

Cousin David wouldn't have cared how Granddaddy used his napkin. He and my granddaddy had grown up together, double first cousins who were as close as brothers. Granddaddy used to tease Cousin David about his prominent nose, saying it would provide plenty of shade on a sunny summer's day. Cousin David teased him back, calling my hefty grandfather "a delicate-looking little thing." Granddaddy had supplied Cousin David with country clothes and boots as a costume for his first acting part, a role in a church play in Louisville.

Other relatives began to arrive and finally Cousin David. He was still a handsome man with a commanding voice like that of his father, Colonel Jacob Wark "Roaring Jake" Griffith, who had led Confederate cavalry charges during the Civil War. It was near Christmas, and Cousin David had brought presents for everyone. His chauffeur, Richard Reynolds, brought them in, wrapped and ribboned boxes in two large shopping bags.

Sitting in Granddaddy's easy chair, his face reddened by the fire blazing in the potbellied stove, Cousin David called out names and presented the gifts, all bought at fashionable New York stores. He presented my aunt Evelyn, perhaps his favorite young cousin, with a silver bracelet from Tiffany's. He had wanted to take her to Hollywood many years before, seeing her as another Mary Pickford, "America's sweetheart," but my grandmother had refused to allow it. He also wrote checks to everyone, my granddaddy and daddy and uncles each receiving one hundred dollars.

Grandmother then announced dinner, and everyone sat down at the long dining table. Halfway through the meal, Cousin David told everyone he planned to marry a young actress named Evelyn Baldwin, who had appeared in his last film, "The Struggle." He said they would be married as soon as his divorce from Linda Arvidson Griffith was granted. The newlyweds planned to live in La Grange for a while as he worked on his autobiography.

"That'll give me a chance to whip you at the pool table," my grandfather quipped.

The dinner was going beautifully, with Cousin David thoroughly enjoying the meal and complimenting my grandmother on her cooking, until the conversation turned to movies.

"I think you're helping the Devil with his work," Grandmother said suddenly, staring at Cousin David.

"I'm sorry you feel that way, Jenny, but I believe my movies are a force for good."

"I can't see how a parade of naked women can improve anyone's morals," Grandmother said.

He managed a faint smile and answered evenly. "I'm afraid you've a narrow view, Jenny."

Cousin David was right, of course, about Grandmother's having a narrow view. She was a religious fanatic. That was her only fault. Even the commonest pleasures—drinking and dancing and smoking—were scarlet sins to her way of thinking. Any woman who smoked was a harlot. Any man who took even a drink of hard liquor was Satan's disciple.

Her fanaticism took some strange paths. Sometimes, before the entire congregation of DeHaven Memorial Baptist Church, she would rattle the family skeletons and ask the congregation to pray for the sinners. In a dark purple dress, her gray hair pulled back severely from her face and wound into a hard bun, she'd clear her throat and start. Her eldest son, Joseph, drank to excess. Her second daughter, Ruth, had married a Catholic! Her words rang out with suffocating force, drowning even the *whoosh* of the palm-shaped fans on a hot summer day. The words became a torrent, madly swirling; but just as quickly the torrent stopped, and she sat down, calmly fanning herself.

Somehow her zealotry never troubled my grandfather. He would either ignore her ranting and raving, or start playing the piano and singing when she began to sermonize.

God rest her soul. She was the best cook in Oldham County.

GRANDMOTHER'S LEMON MERINGUE PIE

Pie Crust
3 cups premium flour
½ level teaspoon baking powder
1 level teaspoon salt
¾-cup lard

Sift together dry ingredients, add a pinch of sugar, and work in lard with knife; then moisten with water. Place dough on a board dusted with flour and roll flat, then put in pie pan. Trim edge and punch holes in bottom and sides to keep it from rising. Bake until done (about 15 minutes at 350). Allow to cool.

Lemon Filling
¾-cup sugar
¾-cup boiling water
1-tablespoon flour
2 egg yolks
3 tablespoons lemon juice
1-teaspoon butter
Grated rind of one lemon

Mix flour and sugar, adding boiling water constantly. Cook for two minutes before adding butter, egg yolks, rind and juice. Pour into piecrust and add meringue. Return to oven and bake until meringue is tinged a soft brown.

Meringue
2 egg whites
1-teaspoon water
2 tablespoons powdered sugar
1-teaspoon lemon juice or ¼-teaspoon vanilla extract

Beat egg whites and water until stiff. Gradually add powdered sugar. Continue whipping and add lemon juice or vanilla extract.

David Wark Griffith, circa 1910.

Mr. & Mrs. Woodson Oglesby and the children and the spotted dog, and
the calf, and the rest of them that are concerned,

How is this about the fat one, Woodson Oglesby being sick?
I knew the last time I saw the delicate looking thing something was
going to happen. We didn't hear anything about it until it was all
over and you were well again. Next time you do anything like this,
let us know about it, so we can be happy too. I sent you a copy of
Leslies Weekly this last week . You can read the junk I am responsi-
ble for, or not, just as you please. The name is no forgery. Woodson,
get the wife to read it, I dont expect you to, and the babies will tell
you what it is about. Dont you puzzle your head. The hair is getting
than enough anyhow, so dont trouble it any more. No, all nonsense
out of the question, when you get this, I'd like you to sit down and
write us a letter, tell us all about yourselves, how the kids are
and anything else you feel like doing. Would like to have seen you
this summer, but of corse, ye had so little time. Hope to do so in
the not too far future. Good morning Mrs. Oglesby, how are you
feeling to-day. Give my regards to the kids. Hoping you the best of
luck,

    Yours handsomely,

         David, also his wife not near so handsome, Linda

Linda says "She dont like that", she thinks she's the handsomest.
Aint it the truth? L.

Pay no attention to the above very foolish communication. David means
well,   only he doesn't know any better'
         Your cousin,
            Linda.

Windemere Court.
348 St. Nicholas Ave., New York.

*This rare, typewritten letter, its envelope postmarked
February 12, 1907, to my grandparents "and the children
and the spotted dog and the calf..." was written by D. W.
Griffith before he became famous. The note at the bottom
of the letter was added by his first wife, actress Linda
Arvidson, whom he married on May 14, 1906. The letter
pokes fun at my grandfather.*

*D.W. Griffith (center, in straw hat) poses with his Oglesby
relatives, including the author's parents, Mary Lee
Wigginton Oglesby and Joseph Woodson Oglesby, Sr.,
(extreme right) after Sunday dinner in La Grange, Ky.*

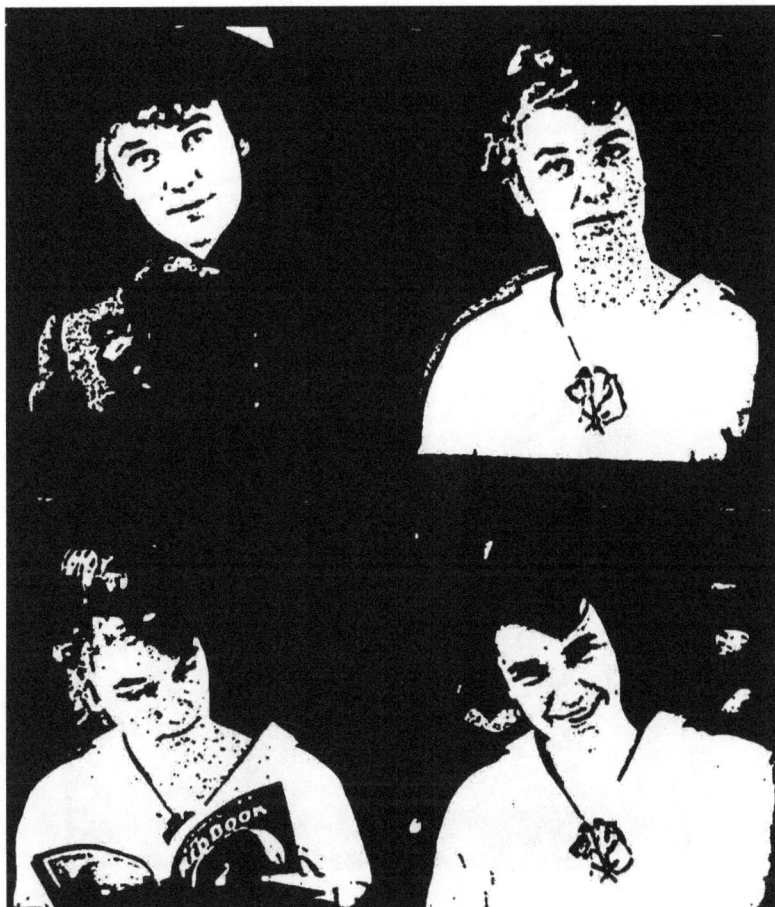

Vignettes of my aunt Evelyn, whom D. W. Griffith wanted to train as a star in silent movies. My grandmother protested so vehemently that it never happened.

My grandfather Woodson Oglesby, left, and D. W. Griffith, shown outside Grandfather's farm home, were life-long chums and double first cousins.

*Grandmother Jenny Oglesby with her three daughters,
from left, Evelyn, Ruth and Nancy Grey.*

The Piano Player

There wasn't anything Rice couldn't do. He played the piano by ear, he drove a taxi, and he was almost as good an Indian wrestler as my daddy. He could swallow a whole pickled egg without blinking an eye. Rice also had a great thirst. He loved the moonshine an old black man who lived in the alley behind our place used to sell. On Saturday nights Rice and my daddy would knock on the old man's door. They'd pay Jim for a jug of moonshine, and then the three of them would commence having a good time.

Jim's place wasn't much more than a shed, but it was very homey and cozy. A big brass bed, so shiny you could see your reflection in the huge foot posts, dominated the room. Bright green-and-white linoleum decorated the floor. On a small bureau sat a blue vase with one artificial rose in it. The pungent smell of kerosene clung to the walls since Jim used kerosene in his stove and in the large, cut-glass lamp that sat on his kitchen table. In one corner of the room stood a battered old piano, given to him—along with the brass bed and the cut-glass lamp—by a rich family he worked for.

Jim loved to hear Rice play that piano. If the moonshine

ran low he'd replace it, so long as Rice kept playing. "Dark Town Strutters Ball" was Jim's favorite piece. Rice's hands were huge and skinny, and they flew up and down the yellowed keyboard of the old upright. He played hard and loud and sometimes sang along as he played. His voice was always hoarse:

"I'll be down to get you in a taxi, honey,

"Better be ready 'bout half past eight...."

Rice's favorite dish was kale greens, cooked slow in plenty of water and seasoned with a slab of jowl bacon, accompanied by a pie platter full of thick yellow cornbread. A lot of times he ate with Jim, since Jim loved kale greens and fatback, too, and knew just how to cook them.

Rice was well-educated, but he never talked about his early life. Nobody knew exactly where he came from or if he had any sisters or brothers. But his manners were beautiful, when he wanted to use them. Sometimes he and my daddy would discuss religion or philosophy.

Daddy had first met Rice at Corso's, a Fifth Street bar where Rice demonstrated his egg-swallowing feats and Daddy reigned as undisputed Indian-wrestling champ. Not long afterward, he invited Rice home for supper. I don't think Mother was too happy about it. But when she met the stranger, she succumbed to his charm just as everyone else did. He came to supper in a nice plaid suit. His shoes were shiny. His dark black hair was slicked down with Dixie Peach and his nails clean. He tousled my hair and showed me how to play tic-tac-toe.

When we all were seated at our dining table, Mother asked Rice if he would give the thanks.

"Yes, ma'am," he said.

They bowed their heads, although I noticed my daddy never closed his eyes.

"Dear Lord, bless this house and this food, and may it nourish our bodies and our souls, in your name, Amen."

Mother was delighted. My father always mumbled, and I was too shy to give thanks yet. But what especially pleased her was the way Rice appreciated her food. He took two helpings of everything—including the country ham she'd fried in generous servings—and cleaned his plate. After dessert, he even helped her clear the table, although she protested, but not too much. My father never helped clear the table.

From that time on, anything Rice did or said was okay by Mother. But what she could never understand was why Rice chose to drive a taxicab and live in a furnished room, when a man with his education and looks and good manners could have had a far better station in life. But she never asked Rice any embarrassing questions. I think she treasured him just as my daddy did and old Jim, the black man.

Rice came often to Sunday dinner, but he never wore out his welcome. Because he was such a good conversationalist and such a thoughtful man as well, he was a treat for Mother. Yet, there'd be long spells when we didn't see him.

"What's happened to Rice?" Mother would ask.

"I don't know, Mary Lee," Daddy would say.

"Have we made him angry?"

My father would look at her with a strange cast to his eyes, because he knew that wasn't so, but he'd answer easily. "No. Rice takes spells of wanting to be to himself."

Just when we were afraid we'd never see Rice again, he'd show up, and he and my daddy would head for Corso's or Carl's Place, a pool parlor. One Saturday night my mother and I went for a walk before bed. As we passed the mouth of the alley, we heard piano music and Rice's loud, hoarse voice:

"I'll be down to get you in a taxi, honey,

"Better be ready 'bout half past eight...."

"Is that Rice singing?" Mother asked, looking into my face.

"Yes, Mama."

"He sounds drunk!" she said.

"Oh, he's just cutting up in Jim's place."

"You mean that old black man who sells moonshine?"

I nodded, looking away. I didn't like to rat on Rice, but I never lied to Mama.

"Is your daddy with them?" she asked.

"Ah, I guess so."

A hurt look pinched her face. "They told me they were going to play billiards."

That was the turning point. After that, it became my mother's mission to save Rice from a life of waste. I think she'd given up on my daddy and that she knew he drank too much and played poker and shot pool. But Rice was salvageable.

The next Sunday, with Rice as the invited guest, Mother staged one of her best Sunday dinners—roast chicken with cornbread dressing, dumplings, green beans, okra, pickled beets, homemade wheat bread and apple pie. She picked this occasion to make an announcement. "I've just met the nicest girl," she said. "She's a librarian."

Neither of the men paid much attention. Rice was finishing his second piece of pie. My father was smoking a cigar.

"Her name is Patricia Waters. I think you'd like her, Rice."

Thoughtfully, Rice chewed a mouthful of pie. "I don't go out very often anymore, Mary," he said. He never used Mother's middle name, Lee. "I'm too busy."

"Seems to me you have plenty of time for *other* things," Mother said.

I knew she would have her way. Through her finagling, Rice met Pat, and right away they hit it off. Mother was pleased with her meddling. But in a way, she was sorry, I think, because Rice didn't come to our place as often, although we received regular reports on him.

Rice left the taxicab job and became a salesman for Montgomery-Ward. The piano in Jim's place gathered dust. My daddy seemed glum. Our Sunday dinners weren't nearly as good. Then came the engraved card that announced Rice and Patricia's forthcoming marriage at Duncan Memorial Chapel in Crestwood.

"I always wanted to marry there," Mother said as she showed my father the card. "It's such a beautiful place."

Daddy glanced at the card. "The wedding's less than two weeks away, Mary Lee. We'll want to get them something."

Mother smiled. "Something very nice. I have some money saved."

Mother bought them a beautiful silver chafing dish, but the couple never received it. The morning of the wedding, Rice disappeared. No one, including the bride-to-be, ever heard from him again.

My mother used a parasol to keep from getting pink-faced on sunny days in those far-gone times when it wasn't lady-like for a Southern girl to have a tan.

The Great Flood

$\mathcal{D}$ay after day after day the rains came, swelling the Ohio River. The sky was sepia colored. Even during daylight hours, motorists drove with their lights on through black curtains of rain, and homemakers burned lamps in windows to dispel the darkness and gloom. The month was January, the year 1937.

When the raging water backed up in storm sewers and covered sidewalks, and the radio carried warnings of possible electrical outages, everyone began to worry. People trimmed the wicks of their kerosene lamps and filled them, and bought candles and flashlights. They began to stock extra canned goods in their cupboards and filled jugs with emergency water supplies. Some families made plans to leave the city; others moved to a higher floor to escape the rising water.

My father came home late one night with the announcement that the water was knee-deep in the grocery store he managed on Market Street, only two blocks from the river. He'd moved what stock he could to storage on high ground in the city's east end and closed the store. My mother and daddy discussed our plight long into the night and decided it would be best if my mother and I took refuge with my aunt Wheeler and Uncle Billy in their home in Pewee Valley, a village some 18 miles east of Louisville, out of the flood plain.

Mother called Aunt Wheeler that night, and early the next day, my uncle Billy drove into town and picked up my mother and me in a black Model A Ford. Uncle Billy was one of my heroes, since he'd ridden with General John Joseph "Blackjack" Pershing into Mexico to try to arrest Pancho Villa. When Uncle Billy returned from the campaign he sulked for days, or so I was told, because they hadn't caught the Mexican bandit.

Daddy decided to stay in town. He was sure the water wouldn't rise much more.

"I wish you'd come with us, Joe," Mother said as she kissed him good-by.

"You worry too much, honey," he said. "I'll be all right. Besides, somebody has to stay here to watch the apartment, and I have to reopen the store as soon as it's possible."

Wearing a heavy rubber raincoat and rubber boots, I followed my mother and uncle out to the car. Through the pelting rain I looked back at my father in the doorway; he was just a smudge, hardly discernible. I suddenly hated the rain; it was separating me from my father.

As we left Louisville, along with hundreds of other fleeing refugees, floodwater the color of ancient pennies came up to the running board of the Model A and threatened to kill the brakes. The car's wipers could barely keep the glass clear as the rain kept assaulting it.

The rain did not follow us into Pewee Valley. It was like entering a new world as we approached the village. I hadn't visited Uncle Billy and Aunt Wheeler in their home since I was much younger, and I didn't remember their place. It was a white frame cottage with Gothic windows and blue shutters and gingerbread woodwork around the porch and eaves. Its roof was dark blue, and a lightning rod rose from its brick chimney. When the car pulled into the gravel driveway, a barking bulldog ran up to greet us—old Susie.

We all gathered around my aunt's round, golden oak table to eat breakfast and to talk about the Louisville flood before Aunt Wheeler left to work her half-day as the village postmistress, and Uncle Billy took off for his job as a mechanic at a Crestwood garage. As my mother cleared the table, I wandered about the house, first looking at all the framed photos crowding the parlor. My maternal grandparents' photos, hand-tinted, smiled back from oval mahogany frames. Both had died before I was old enough to know them, but seeing the photos caused me to ask questions about them. My grandfather Dewitt Clinton Wigginton, my mother told me, had owned a cotton mill, which had been passed down to him from his father. His hobby was Civil War history. He had married my grandmother when he was forty and she was only twenty. His brother Rufus had been known for his fiddlin'. He played at all the community dances. There were also photos of my uncle Billy in his army uniform, taken somewhere in Mexico, and of my mother and father on their wedding day. I didn't recognize them. I was born 10 years into their marriage.

On that first afternoon in Pewee Valley, I discovered Foley's General Store in the heart of the village. I lingered at the huge candy case where purple jawbreakers and black licorice sticks and banana squares and red-hots and Snow White suckers filled box after box. It was hard for me to make up my mind how to spend the penny Uncle Billy had given me before he'd left for work. Finally, I selected a licorice stick because I figured it would last longer than a jawbreaker or banana square.

In the middle of the store squatted a potbellied stove, its fat belly glowing red, a ring of Foley's customers gathered around it. Farmers or villagers, the menfolk were propped back in straight chairs, their feet braced on the stove's fender, discussing in somber tones the Louisville flood. Their voices were hushed, like those of people paying their last respects at a funeral home. Their talk made me feel uneasy about my daddy.

That night Daddy called and told us that he and my uncle Jim, a wallpaper hanger, had locked up our apartment and moved into the vacant attic apartment above ours because of the rising water. They planned to sleep on old mattresses and to use kerosene lamps for light; the electricity had failed.

When my mother called my daddy back the next morning, she didn't get through; the telephone lines were down. Wan and shaken, she rushed into the parlor and turned on the Philco radio for flood news. The WHAS radio reports were ominous. Red Cross boats were crisscrossing the city in search of stranded people. The streets of central and western Louisville were canals. Numerous deaths from drowning and pneumonia or flu were reported. Whenever a Red Cross boat was dispatched, the radio announcer gave the address where the boat was being sent. My mother kept hoping she'd hear our address—1023 South Third Street. She stayed by the radio hour after hour listening for that address. It never came.

To keep my mind off my daddy, I explored the village. With Susie running ahead of me sniffing trees or barking hellos to villagers, I started up the L & N railroad tracks. By following the tracks, I knew I couldn't get lost—all I had to do was go back the way I'd come. I wandered up Peace Lane and discovered a stable behind one of the houses and made friends with an old horse that allowed me to pet him. I stopped to peer through the panes of a greenhouse where the bright red and yellow and pink blossoms made me feel that spring had already arrived. The whole world seemed mine now. I was free to go wherever I wanted. There were no traffic lights in Pewee Valley, few automobiles, no noisy trolley cars—and what's more, no school to attend.

Throughout that afternoon and evening, we still heard no news of my father and uncle. No one slept well that night. Mother kept rising to turn on the radio, and from the parlor alcove where I slept on a small daybed, I could see the yellow glow of its dial, like a huge lightning bug in the dark, and hear its crackling; the reception was poor.

During my explorations the next day, I came upon a house of mystery, sitting all alone at the end of a long lane of locust trees. It seemed abandoned. With hesitation I started up the long lane. As I drew closer, I could see reflections of the sentinel locusts in the tall front windows of the house. A breeze stirred and whistled through the cracks of the doors and windows, making an eerie sound, almost like that of a crying child. As the wind died, I tiptoed closer and looked through a front window into the parlor. All the furniture was shrouded in white sheets. The hands and pendulum of a grandfather clock were still.

Later, my aunt told me I had been visiting The Locust, once the home of the Little Colonel, made famous in a series of books written by Annie Fellows Johnston, who had lived in a village house called The Beeches until her death in 1931. The present owners of The Locust had closed the house for the winter and gone to Florida, not to return until the Kentucky spring.

That night, as we anxiously huddled around the radio—Aunt Wheeler and Uncle Billy and my mother and I—to hear the flood news, I prayed to Jesus to help my daddy and uncle. The radio announcer instructed people in the flooded areas to go to their rooftops or to wave from their windows so they'd be spotted by the Red Cross rescue boats. We wondered if Daddy and Uncle Jim had even heard about the Red Cross boats since they'd lost their electricity. Were they warm? The temperatures were dropping. Did they still have enough food? How did they spend the long, dark nights, death and misery surrounding them?

The water kept rising. Thousands were homeless. Businesses and factories had shut down. A great lake covered all of downtown Louisville.

"I just know something's happened to Joe," Mother said over and over as we listened to the crackling radio reports.

"He's an old country boy, Mary Lee," Uncle Billy said. "He can take care of himself."

"I worry about Jim," Aunt Wheeler said. "He's so thin. He's never been well anyway, ever since Bobbie died." Bobbie, Uncle Jim's wife, had died of consumption only three years after their marriage.

Two days after the river had crested, I heard gravel pop in the driveway. I stopped playing with my uncle Billy's old telegraph machine in the parlor and ran to the front door to see who was coming. When I pushed open the door, I saw my daddy beside a muddy Plymouth sedan, stretching his long legs. He looked so tall, in black trousers and a heavy white cardigan sweater. A gray cap sat lopsided on his head. He smiled broadly when he saw me. Beside him stood my uncle Jim, who looked skinny in a pinstriped suit that belonged to my daddy. He was smiling so hard he looked foolish, or drunk. Someone inside the car passed their topcoats and suitcases out to them.

I started running. I fell down and skinned my knees on gravel and they bled, but I didn't even notice. My daddy was home.

*The 1937 flood inundated all of downtown Louisville,
including the city's hub at Fourth and Broadway streets
(above), and vast portions of the city's west and south
ends. About 230,000 of the city's 350,000 residents were
evacuated, and 90 people died.*

*The statue of Abraham Lincoln, at the main branch of the
Louisville Free Public Library, appears to be standing on
water during the Great Flood of 1937.*

My uncle Billy arrived in this 1928 Ford Model A to take my mother and me to Pewee Valley as the Great Flood invaded our Louisville home.

My uncle Billy (William Chandler) rode with General Joseph "Blackjack" Pershing in pursuit of Mexican bandit Pancho Villa.

Sweethearts: My aunt Wheeler and uncle Billy before their marriage.

My aunt Wheeler Chandler, named after a Confederate general, was the first postmistress of Pewee Valley, Ky.

*During the flood, my mother and I stayed with my aunt
and uncle in their gingerbread house similar to this one in
Pewee Valley.*

Annie Fellows Johnston in her home, The Beeches, in Pewee Valley. She wrote The Little Colonel *books, made into movies starring Shirley Temple.*

Kate Matthews' famous photograph of Hattie Cochran, the Pewee Valley girl who was the model for the main character in The Little Colonel *books.*

The Locust, home of the Little Colonel.

The Belated Christmas Gift

Christmas of 1938 promised to be a memorable one. My mother had been working part-time as a telephone operator, so we had some extra dollars to make the holidays merrier.

"We'll have the best Christmas ever," Mother said. "I'll cook a goose, and we'll have scalloped potatoes and cranberry sauce and apple pie. I'll invite Wheeler and Billy." Aunt Wheeler and Uncle Billy lived in Pewee Valley. We'd taken refuge in their home during the horrible Louisville flood in January of the previous year.

"Goody!" I said. "Maybe Uncle Billy will bring his telegraph set, and I can play with it."

"I'll ask him when I call Wheeler with the invitation," Mother said.

For weeks I had been nurturing a secret wish that I'd receive a Defender BB gun for Christmas. My best friend, Herbie Baird, already owned one. He let me fire his; we lined up toy soldiers and shot them down. But it wasn't the same as having my own.

I still halfway believed in Santa Claus. I was afraid not to. Herbie had scoffed at the idea that the Easter Bunny delivered colored eggs and candies and, as a result, had gotten nothing but one black jelly bean this past Easter. I wasn't about to run that risk.

I dropped a hint about the BB gun to my mother, who I figured had a straight line to Santa Claus.

"Those guns are expensive," Mother said. "I think they cost five dollars."

"Yes, ma'am, but they last forever, and BBs are only 15 cents a package. I can pay for them with my allowance or the money I make shoveling snow."

"You won't be shooting squirrels, I hope."

"No, ma'am."

Four days before Christmas, Daddy brought home a cedar tree, and we erected it near the bay window in the living room. We decorated it with tinsel and silvery ornaments with red and green and yellow stripes, and one tiny, sparkly reindeer. Mother fashioned a gold star from silky ribbon from the dime store and affixed it atop the tree. It bore no lights, but I thought it was the grandest Christmas tree I'd ever seen. I lay on the floor near it at night and aimed the beams of a flashlight through its branches, making the tinsel and ornaments glisten.

Mother began her preparations for the Christmas dinner, buying oranges and apples and flour and spices from a neighborhood market. Daddy supplied the fat goose from the meat market on Jefferson Street where he worked. Since school was already out, I was enjoying all the fringe benefits of the Christmas holiday, such as snowball fights, sledding down Iroquois hill and drinking hot apple cider at night while I admired the Christmas tree. But all this merriment came to a halt two nights before Christmas when my daddy came home from work and began to complain of sharp pains in his left arm. He also said his jaw ached and that he could barely chew his pork chops at supper.

"Let me see your arm, Joe," my mother said.

Reluctantly, he rolled up his sleeve and revealed a long,

purplish streak that started at his thumb and rose past his elbow.

"Did you cut yourself?" Mother asked.

"It was nothing. I just nicked my thumb on a meat saw."

"Did you treat it with iodine?"

"Nah. I just ran cold water over it."

"It's infected."

It got worse. By midnight, my daddy could not open his mouth. Mother decided he needed to go to the Jewish Hospital emergency room. Digging into her Christmas money, she extracted a five-dollar bill and went to the landlord's to call a cab. Daddy was so weak now he could barely stand.

"I'll be back as soon as I can," Mother told me. "Don't worry."

Daddy tried to speak but couldn't. He had trouble managing even a faint smile for me.

That night I paced the apartment and kept looking out the windows. A light snow was falling. The traffic light at the corner changed from green to yellow to red regularly, but there was almost no traffic to heed it; it was little more than an ornament on that snowy morning. Somewhere in our apartment building the notes of "Silent Night" rang out from a radio. I sprayed the Christmas tree with the beam of my flashlight, but the magic was gone. It was just a dumb old cedar tree, already drooping and shedding.

About 6 a.m. Mother returned, awakening me. Her face was as pale as the falling snow. "The doctors are very worried about your father, Joe. They're giving him blood transfusions. He has lockjaw."

"What's that?" I asked.

"It's a serious infection. I must get back to him now, but I wanted to check on you. Are you okay?"

"I guess," I said gloomily.

I wouldn't know until years later that my daddy had

been close to dying that night. He didn't return home until three days after Christmas. Mother had cancelled the
Christmas dinner with my aunt and uncle but cooked the
goose for the three of us and made a thick, juicy apple pie.

Santa Claus didn't make it to our place that Christmas;
he was in the hospital. But the day he came home was the
best Christmas gift I ever received.

A Taste of the Country

*I*t was my cousin James Rae's idea that the two of us soak up the pleasures of country living on my aunt Susie and Uncle Cap's farm near Crestwood. "We'll go fishing and play croquet and take walks into town for cold soft drinks," he promised. "Aunt Susie's been wanting us to visit."

We took a bus to Crestwood and walked from town the half mile to my aunt Susie's place. Rae, a few years older than I, carried the suitcase we were sharing. Aunt Susie was rocking on the porch and fanning herself when we started up the gravel driveway. When she saw us, she smiled and started off the porch to greet us.

"You boys look so hot," she said, taking our bag. "I've made a pitcher of lemonade for you. Just rest a spell on the porch. I'll be right back."

We slid into the porch swing and began to glide to and fro and suck in the warm, sweet smells of summer. Cicadas were sounding off all around us, and occasionally a car would pass on the blacktop highway, but it was basically quiet. I was used to the clang of streetcars, the blare of car horns, the sounds of peddlers vending their wares ... "Get your strawberries, red, ripe strawberries!" ... sirens, screaming kids spraying each other with garden hoses—city sounds.

Soon Aunt Susie returned with lemonade in a clear pitcher in which swam large chunks of ice and slices of lemon in cistern water. I drank two glasses straight down. James Rae drank only one glass; he didn't particularly like lemonade. His taste ran more to Kool-Aid or Nehi orange.

"I have to string some pole beans for supper," Aunt Susie said. "You boys do whatever you like. Your uncle Cap's working in the garden, and your cousin Ruth's in the barn with the new kittens; they might interest you."

"Yes, ma'am," we said.

We wandered toward the barn, which sat some 300 yards diagonally behind the large frame farmhouse with the wraparound porch. My cousin Ruth, who was a bit "touched in the head," as they used to say, but who had managed to earn a high school diploma and could play the piano by ear, was tending to the kittens when we entered the barn. She looked up. "Why, if it isn't James Rae and Little Joe!" she cried out, rushing to us and kissing Rae on the cheek. "What a nice surprise. I didn't really think you'd come visit us for a whole week. Want to see the kittens?"

"Sure," I said.

I really wasn't too interested in cats. I liked dogs—the bigger, the better. But I didn't want to hurt Ruth's feelings.

She plucked a gray kitten with blue eyes from his blanket and displayed him. "He's only three days old," she explained. "Sleeps most of the time."

"Where's the mama cat?" James Rae asked, making conversation.

"She don't pay much attention to her little ones," Ruth said. "Wanders off. Of course, she's got business to attend to."

"What kind of business?" I asked, most curious.

"Oh, Queenie's our ratter. Keeps the rats out of the

corn and hay. Eats them sometimes."

I was beginning to learn something about farm life. "Has she had kittens before?" I asked.

"She's had twelve litters."

"What'd you do with all those cats?" James Rae asked.

"Pa delivers then to heaven."

Now, I didn't really picture my uncle Cap as a spiritual or even religious-type person. He was a man of few words and snappish when he did speak. He was small but as tough as bull hide, his face weathered by sun and rain, his hands rough and chapped from hard work in his garden and tobacco allotment. Rae told me that my uncle Jim had once seen him at the Savoy Burlesque House in Louisville ogling the young dancers at a Saturday matinee. While my aunt Susie was a regular churchgoer, Uncle Cap wasn't. He apparently preferred a chunk of chewing tobacco or a walk into Crestwood to the ordeals of Sunday worship.

At any rate, as we started back to the house, Aunt Susie reappeared on the porch. "Would you boys like some nice fried chicken for supper?" she asked.

Yummy. Yummy. I loved chicken drumsticks. "Sure would," I said.

"My mouth's watering already," James Rae said.

We were playing a game of croquet with Ruth—sliding easily into the rhythms of country living—when we heard a loud squawking in the backyard.

"What's happening?" I said, lifting my mallet and staring toward the squawking.

"That's a chicken got loose," Ruth said, with authority.

"Let's go see," said James Rae.

When we rounded the house, we saw my aunt Susie proudly displaying the chicken she'd caught. "Nice and plump, isn't he?" she said. He was a handsome creature—a rooster. "Do you boys want to watch?" Aunt Susie asked.

I didn't know what she meant. Rae did, and he was cruel not to tell me. "Sure," he said.

She grasped the protesting rooster by his head and spun him around, faster and faster, until his body flew free of his head. The red-plumed head was left in her hand, little dark eyes staring up at the blue sky. But the body thrashed all over the yard, painting the grass red with rooster blood. Finally the heart stopped, and the rooster lay still, blood oozing from the hole where his neck had been separated from the rest of him.

I ran into high weeds and lost my lunch and then became angry with Rae. "Why didn't you tell me?" I asked.

"I thought you knew."

I guess I knew remotely that chickens were killed for their meat, but the full reality of how a chicken got to a farmer's dinner table hadn't entered my consciousness until that summer afternoon.

Come suppertime, I wasn't hungry. I nibbled at the pole beans and ate two sticks of cornbread.

"What's wrong with your appetite, boy?" Uncle Cap demanded.

"I'm a light eater, Uncle Cap, especially in the summer."

"You could use some meat on your bones, boy," he snapped.

The next day, Uncle Cap allowed James Rae and me to run his tractor.

I was beginning to like Uncle Cap a little. As I sat high on the tractor's iron seat, he showed me how to shift gears. I was soon scooting along at 10 miles an hour, breezing up one side of my uncle's huge vegetable garden.

When we returned the tractor to the barn, I looked for the kittens. I looked everywhere. Uncle Cap was refilling the tractor with gas when I approached him. "What happened to all the kittens, Uncle Cap?"

"Too many mouths to feed," he snapped.

I didn't understand, but he was too gruff to be asked any more questions. That evening, I asked Aunt Susie about the kittens. She grimaced. "If I tell you, will you promise never to tell Ruth?" she said.

"Yes, ma'am."

"Cap drowns them in the creek behind the farm."

I was shocked. My uncle was a cat killer. "Why would he do that?"

"We don't need but one ratter. It's expensive to feed a bunch of cats."

"Why not give them away?"

"Nobody in these parts is looking for another cat."

I kept thinking of that sweet little gray kitten with blue eyes, and I kept hearing the rooster's squawking before he was killed.

"Would you mind if we went back to Louisville pretty soon?" I asked James Rae that night. We were lying on our cots on the long side porch of the farmhouse. The stars were out. Honeysuckle and jasmine scented the air.

"Shoot fire, no. I'm bored to tears."

We had intended to spend a whole week on the farm, but we lasted only two days.

Aunt Susie in the front yard of her farm home near Crestwood, KY.

Black Market Spy

*W*AR!

I'd seen the word often enough in smaller type in my U.S. history books, and I knew about the Revolutionary War, the War of 1812, the Civil War and the Spanish-American War, but I'd never seen the word in nearly foot-high letters on the front page of the local newspaper. The urgency and alarm in the newsboy's voice as he hawked the newspapers emphasized the deadly message: "Extra! Extra! Read all about it. Congress declares war on Japan."

I was headed home from school the day after the Japanese bombed Pearl Harbor when I encountered the newsboy at the corner of First and Kentucky streets. With a nickel I'd saved for a Babe Ruth bar, I bought one of the newspapers. I read every line on the front page before I reached home.

Sure, the whole neighborhood and the school were abuzz with war talk, and most every family kept a radio tuned for further details. My teachers had devoted the day to the subject. But it wasn't until I saw the tall, black, Bodoni bold headline—*WAR!* —that I fully understood the gravity and horror of it all. Those gigantic black letters made war official and final to me in a way no spoken words possibly could.

Everyone began to make sacrifices for the war effort. Mrs. Rosalee Spechter donated her ornate iron fence, the only one in the neighborhood with an iris design, to the government's scrap-iron drive, sure it would end up as a tank or airplane. My mother, who was deathly afraid of doctors and needles, gave a pint of blood each month to the Red Cross. Nobody complained about the rationing of gasoline, meat, sugar, butter and other items because it helped the guys and gals in service. The ration book, issued to each head of family, became a fixed feature of the war years.

My cousin James Rae signed up for the Navy. He had to have his father's consent since he was only seventeen. He came by our house and told us, and I thought that was really something. I just knew he'd be on a PT boat or a destroyer and drop mines on Japanese submarines or shoot Zeroes out of the sky.

When James Rae left for boot training at Great Lakes Naval Station, everybody in the family became even more patriotic. My uncle Jim, James Rae's father, took a construction job at the Jeffersonville Boat Works, which was making LSDs—landing craft for the Navy. My aunt Wheeler and Uncle Billy, who never had any children of their own, placed a star flag, usually displayed by mothers of enlisted people, in their parlor window and planted a victory garden. My daddy bought defense bonds every week.

We had a Philco radio that was equipped with short wave. By carefully adjusting its knobs, we sometimes picked up London at night and the voice of the BBC, with those horrible, tense, bleak reports of the London blitz.

I had to do something for the war effort, too, so I joined the neighborhood Civil Defense team becoming a "messenger." I was so proud of my CD armband that I sometimes wore it to school, and I always took part in the practice air raids.

The Victory letters from James Rae came to us on tissue-thin paper, envelopes with a red, white and blue border. All of us read his letters several times. In one of them he promised me a Japanese rifle since he was in the Pacific theater at that time. I went to sleep thinking about the rifle—how I'd shine it and where I'd hang it, how I'd "show off" with it. I'm sure I never thought of *how* James Rae would get the rifle. I used to love to go into the Third Avenue Arcade and fire the air rifle that shot down Tojo's ugly mug.

On Sundays Uncle Jim would come by for dinner. Usually, he was a bit tipsy and wore a silly smile. Every now and then he'd duck into the bathroom and take a nip of Sweet Lucy, his generic name for any number of cheap wines he favored. When his mood was sufficiently maudlin, he'd bend into my face, blowing wine fumes, and make his request. "How about playing my song, Little Joe?" he'd say.

"Okay."

I'd seat myself at the piano and do a few exercises while Uncle Jim stood behind me. I'd breeze through my sheet music until I found his song—"Bellbottom Trousers"—about a sailor. As I banged it out on the piano, Uncle Jim would sing. If he'd had too much to drink, he'd break out in tears before I finished the song. But usually he struggled through to the end. Then I'd leave him alone with a dreamy look in his eyes as he relaxed in a fat easy chair until Mother announced dinner.

At the time, Uncle Sam was trying to crack down on the Black Market in this country. At first I didn't understand what the Black Market was. When I did I became a zealot, hoping to uncover someone who was cheating on rationing coupons or paying double the cost of something to avoid having to shell out any ration stamps for it.

On Saturdays I helped out as a bagger at my daddy's grocery store, so *maybe* I would catch a customer trying to buy more meat or sugar or coffee or butter than he had coupons for. But Anabelle, the cashier, was very efficient; and if a customer didn't have enough coupons to match his order, she'd inform him of this in a nice way. Probably her efficiency cost my daddy money, but at least it kept his ration-coupon account with the government in good order.

After a number of Saturdays trying to catch a black-market crook in the customer line at my daddy's grocery, I gave up. I was about to resign as a Black Market investigator when one Sunday I went with my daddy to buy some gasoline for our Chevrolet. After we pulled into the service station, Daddy began to act suspiciously. He seemed edgy. Straightening his tie, he got out of the car and walked toward its rear. I watched him in the rearview mirror. When the station owner finished pumping gas into the tank, I saw Daddy hand the man a five-dollar bill—*and no coupons*! The man never bothered to fish for change either, although I knew the bill wasn't nearly that much. Gasoline was only about twenty-nine cents a gallon.

As we pulled out of the station, Daddy started to act like himself again. He was easy-going and friendly.

"What's wrong with you?" he suddenly asked.

I hadn't opened my mouth since we'd pulled out of the station, and I'd edged as close to the door as possible.

"Nothin'," I said.

But for days I brooded. *My own daddy* was dealing in the Black Market. I thought about turning him in but couldn't. I loved him too much. Besides, I didn't even know *where* to turn in a Black Market dealer.

Finally, James Rae got a leave. He didn't bring me a rifle but a Japanese flag, and I hung it in my room. I tried to pump war stories out of him, but he skirted the subject. Instead, he talked about movies. He seemed to know the name of every character actor in Hollywood and could go on about movies for hours. Once, he saw seven different movies in a single day.

One night, as we sat swinging on the back porch in the cool of the evening drinking cherry Kool-Aid, I told him about what Daddy had done. I'd never told another soul.

He laughed.

"But the Black Market hurts the war effort," I said.

"We get everything we need," he said.

"Don't you think what Daddy did was wrong?"

"He probably needed some extra gas so you all could visit your grandmother. I don't see anything so wrong with that."

"I guess not," I said.

If James Rae said so, I figured it was all right. After all, he'd been dodging real Jap bullets.

My cousin James Rae Wigginton at boot camp at Great Lakes, Michigan, 1942.

Mrs. Rosalee Spechter, who gave her ornate iron fence to the scrap-metal drive during World War II.

The Murder Suspect

$\mathcal{V}$erna Garr Taylor, a young widow, was considered the prettiest woman in La Grange. She was also among the wealthiest citizens of that little Kentucky town. She owned the only laundry there and two houses. Her customers included the cadets of the Kentucky Military Institute, which lacked its own laundry.

I remember her only dimly, catching a glimpse of her one day in downtown La Grange. My mother nodded at her in passing, as was the custom in small towns, and then remarked, when Mrs. Taylor was out of hearing distance: "Isn't she a fashion plate?" I had no idea what my mother was talking about. My main interest was to get back to my aunt Lily's place, where we were visiting, for some cold lemonade.

Mrs. Taylor bought her clothes in the best shops in Louisville. She played bridge and drank a cocktail now and then. She was "modern" for her day, running the family business after her husband's death and living an independent existence.

My cousin Chester Woolfolk, Aunt Lily's son, worked

for Mrs. Taylor. He drove the laundry's delivery truck right up to the time of her murder. Some townspeople thought he was in love with her. A few believed he, not General Henry H. Denhardt, who was charged with her murder, killed Verna on a cold November night in 1936 on a lonely road some 12 miles east of La Grange, just outside the Oldham County line. She'd been shot through the chest and her body thrown into a ditch.

My cousin Chester was never the same after Verna's murder, my mother used to say. "Chester was always peculiar," Mother once told me, "but after Verna was murdered, he hardly spoke a word to anybody; crossed to the other side of the street if he saw a relative or friend approaching."

When I was older I decided to investigate the murder. I think my true mission was to clear Chester's name. I was always fond of him, although he never said two-dozen words to me in his lifetime. He was a reed thin, unassuming person who smoked Camels. I guess I liked him because he played the saxophone so beautifully. Sometimes when we visited Aunt Lily and Uncle Parm, who lived in a huge brick house two blocks from Main Street, we'd hear Chester playing "Anything Goes" or "Stardust" in his room. Occasionally, he'd join the rest of us in a game of croquet on the vast lawn at Aunt Lily's. He played a mean game of croquet.

My research revealed that a desperate team of defense attorneys for General Denhardt had attempted to create a "love triangle," with Chester as the other man in Mrs. Taylor's life. The three lawyers concocted a scenario in which Chester had followed the general and Verna that icy November night, and when the general was inside a farmhouse making a phone call, after the couple's car broke down, Chester killed Verna.

Nobody in a sober frame of mind swallowed the defense attorneys' flight of fantasy. There was no proof Chester was ever romantically involved with Mrs. Taylor. He'd worked for her and given her two daughters saxophone lessons; that was all.

A carnival atmosphere prevailed in New Castle, the county seat of Henry County, the first day of General Denhardt's trial. A hillbilly singer and a snake charmer entertained the street crowd. Local Baptist women set up a refreshment stand near the courthouse. The courtroom, on the second floor, was packed. Fearing they'd lose their seats if they left for lunch, some spectators had their food hoisted to them in baskets through the second-floor windows.

The trial attracted journalists from all over the country and even a London, England, newspaper reporter because the defendant, General Denhardt, was such a prominent figure. He'd headed the Kentucky National Guard and directed the attempt to rescue Floyd Collins, who'd been trapped in Sand Cave—another event that drew national attention to the Bluegrass State. He was a war hero and a former lieutenant governor of Kentucky. He and Verna were engaged; the night she was murdered, she was wearing the diamond ring he'd given her. But she'd told her daughters, who disapproved of him, that she intended to break the engagement.

Experts testifying at the trial stated that General Denhardt's gun had killed Mrs. Taylor; that blood on his coat matched hers; and that paraffin tests of his hands proved he'd fired a gun recently, although he claimed he hadn't fired one in six months.

Despite the strong circumstantial evidence against Denhardt, the jury, composed of eleven tobacco farmers and a filling-station operator, deadlocked. Probably most of them had a hard time believing such a prominent person—a war hero and former lieutenant-governor of the commonwealth—could commit a cold-blooded murder, especially in view of his protestations that "I loved her too much to murder her."

The jury's failure to return a guilty charge against General Denhardt enraged Mrs. Taylor's brothers—Dr. E. S. Garr, Roy Garr and Jack Garr. They swore revenge. The moonlit night before the second trial was to begin in Shelby County, the Garr brothers shot General Denhardt to death as he started toward his hotel in the company of one of his lawyers, Rodes K. Myers.

A jury freed the brothers.

A few years after the sensational murder cases, Chester joined the Air Force. When he returned to La Grange, he opened the town's first dry cleaners, a business akin to Mrs. Taylor's. He had acquired her penchant for making money as well. As his dry-cleaning business prospered, he began buying real estate throughout the county. At his death, he was one of the wealthiest persons in Oldham County.

A family vacation photo of Verna Garr Taylor, shot to death on a lonely Kentucky road—one of the most sensational murders in the state's history.

General Henry H. Denhardt was charged with the murder of his fiancée, Verna Garr Taylor.

General Henry H. Denhardt tried to implicate my cousin,
Chester Woolfolk, in the murder of La Grange socialite,
Verna Garr Taylor.

This Courier-Journal photograph shows General Henry H. Denhardt as he lay in the vestibule of the Armstrong Hotel in Shelbyville, KY, after being gunned down by Verna Garr Taylor's brothers.

A Ride in the Paddy Wagon

Every Sunday my daddy gave me my allowance of thirty-five cents, a hefty amount in those days. I nearly always spent most of it on movies and comic books. In the summer I'd supplement my allowance by pulling grass from sidewalk cracks or by running errands for neighbors. This money, too, was spent on my great escapes—movies and comics—and candy bars or popcorn.

My usual companion at the Sunday movies was Kenny. Sunday admission was two for fifteen cents. I'd supply the dime and Kenny tossed in a nickel. We'd usually share the cost of a ten-cent box of buttered popcorn and buy our own candy bars—a Butterfinger or Snickers or Babe Ruth. There were always two movies at least, sometimes three on the Sunday card, plus a serial—Buck Rogers or the Green Hornet or Flash Gordon. We always sat up front, so close we could almost reach out and touch the butt end of Gene Autry's six-shooter.

I loved that movie house. In it I flew from my own body into the Green Hornet's ... I jumped from the second story of saloons onto a horse's back to chase a villain ... I walked behind Stanley through the heart of Africa ... I matched wits with Charlie Chan. It always jarred me to come out of the cool blackness of the Towers into the heat of a summer afternoon, where the glare was blinding and the sidewalks still hot.

It was a long walk home, especially in winter. The only thing that brightened it was the prospect of stopping at Third Avenue Drugs to look over the comic books. I'd browse through an *Archie*, a *Superman*, a *Batman* or a *Captain Marvel* before making my final choice, spending my last dime for one more flight of fantasy before the reality of Monday morning struck, which meant school three-quarters of the year. My love for movies, a kind of addiction, combined with my hatred of school—except for study hall, when I'd go to the library and read novels—eventually got me into big trouble. In junior high school, I began *cutting* school to go to the movies. My friend Blackie and I cut together. We followed a network of alleys all the way from Halleck Hall to downtown, staying off the streets to avoid being spotted by cops.

We always took our time, since the movies didn't start until ten-thirty or eleven o'clock. Sometimes we stopped at a snowball stand to buy a cherry or strawberry or maybe a lime snowball—a ball of chipped ice soaked with a tasty syrup. Sometimes we sidetracked and climbed the high brick wall into Cave Hill Cemetery. (The guards didn't allow little boys not accompanied by adults onto the grounds.) We loved feeding bread to the swans and geese on the main lake, watching our reflections in the dark, oval pool. Once we climbed far up the mouth of one of the caves in the cemetery. The opening was so narrow we had to stay in a bent position, straddling a small stream. The cave was cool and still, and we imagined that was how it felt inside one of the large Gothic mausoleums above us.

We also play-acted on the stage of the Greek theater, where the dedication ceremonies for the Civil War dead had been conducted. Around us the small stone grave markers of the Union dead stretched as far as we could see. As in life, the Confederate dead were separate from the Union dead. Their markers were in a field farther down and on the other side of the cemetery lane.

The tombstones carried only a name and a regiment number. Together, Blackie and I recited the famous lines from Theodore O'Hara's poem inscribed on a bronze plaque fronting the soldiers' field:

"*On Fame's eternal camping ground*
Their silent tents are spread
And Glory guards, with solemn round,
The bivouac of the dead."

On a rainy or snowy day, we avoided the cemetery and headed straight for the Cathedral of the Assumption in downtown Louisville to stay warm and cozy until the movie houses opened. Nobody ever stared at us in the church. The worshippers all seemed too engrossed in their own affairs, their heads lowered as they prayed.

The cathedral was awe-inspiring and mysterious. The brightly painted eyes of plaster saints seemed to follow us. The Latin of the Mass rang in our ears with a magical power. On sunny days, the stained-glass windows cast colored rays onto the dark pews and tiled floor.

But our days of meandering through alleys, chomping on fruity snowballs, and exploring the church and cemetery while other kids wrestled algebra and tried to conjugate Latin verbs were about to come to an end. That last day was a rainy one, appropriately enough. We'd gotten into the Ohio Theater by telling the cashier we were students at St. Mary Magdalene, off for the day because it was a Holy Day of Obligation. We were watching a Johnny Mack Brown western when suddenly the house lights came on. Blackie spilled his popcorn as he dived under the seats in the next row, while Sam, an older kid who'd cut school with us that day, took off like a gazelle for the exit.

When I turned around in my seat to find out what was causing all the excitement, I saw blue everywhere—cops coming up both aisles. I thought maybe a bank robber had run into the theatre. But the cops weren't after big-time crooks. They were looking for little boys cutting school.

Blackie and I rode to the police station in a paddy wagon, all the way proclaiming our innocence. We almost talked the sergeant into believing us until he decided to check out our story with the principal of St. Mary Magdalene.

When my daddy picked me up at the police station late that afternoon, I couldn't even look him in the eye. After that, I didn't cut school anymore.

"Buttons"

His skin was the color of Eastern Kentucky coal, and he wore a frozen smile, like a jagged-tooth Jack-o-Lantern's. His nickname was "Buttons" because he displayed a variety of colorful tin buttons on his coat and vest, advertising political candidates, foods and beverages and business establishments.

Buttons, whose true name was Oliver Crowe, lived in a small frame shack without plumbing or electricity that had once been a chicken house on a farm near La Grange, which is where he milked the cows, tended the garden and helped bring in the tobacco crop in return for his housing and free vegetables from the garden and an occasional slab of fatback to season his mustard and kale greens and pole beans. Buttons had served in the infantry in World War I—in the trenches—one of the few black men from Oldham County to enter the Army. He went to war a bright young man. He returned a cripple, not in body but in mind. He suffered from shell shock, an affliction that followed him to his grave. But he loved company and he liked to smoke—Camels and Chesterfields were his favorite cigarettes. After his small Army disability pension expired every month, he was reduced to cadging cigarettes in the town square.

My first encounter with Buttons happened one hot June

day. It was a Saturday, and my daddy asked me if I'd like to walk into town for a cherry Coke. *Silly question.* We were visiting my grandmother, whose place was about a three-block walk from the drugstore on Main Street. As we headed up the cracked sidewalk, the smell of the tar road, melting like ice cream in the blazing sun, teased my nostrils—a smell I loved. Melting tar meant summertime, and summertime meant freedom.

An L & N (the initials standing for Louisville and Nashville) freight train was passing through downtown, heading east up the Main Street tracks, so we had to wait to cross to the Rexall Drugstore. The railway signal was flashing red and clanging, and some young rednecks, who'd pulled up at the crossing, were cutting up in the bed of a Chevy pickup truck. There must have been five or six of them, and they were all nearly black from the sun, the whites of their eyes somehow scary by contrast. They had bulging arm muscles, made so by hard farm work.

Finally, the caboose rattled past. Sunlight striking the exposed tracks cut like daggers into my eyes, and I hurried with my daddy into the coolness of the drugstore, ripe with the pleasant aromas of the soda fountain and cosmetics section. Daddy and I sat on adjoining stools at the marble counter, and he ordered two cherry Cokes. I felt important sitting there with my daddy in that cool place, seeing my reflection in the mirror behind the counter. I was wearing a new pair of seersucker knickers that added to my sense of well-being.

As we sipped our cherry Cokes and chomped on the crushed ice—a great balm on such a hot day—the rednecks we'd seen in the truck burst into the store. They were loud and boisterous.

"You sell liquor here, mister?" their leader asked Mr. McDowell, the druggist.

"You must be a stranger, mister. Oldham County's as

dry as an old heifer's teats."

"Where can we get something to drink besides a sissy Coke?" another of the farmhands asked, glaring at my daddy and me.

"There's a place just across the Oldham/Jefferson county line on the La Grange Road that sells beer."
They left without thanking Mr. McDowell and banged the door behind them.

"Summer help," my father said. "They're not Oldham County boys. Oldham County boys don't act that way."

We finished our cherry Cokes and left. The June heat smacked us in the face—waves of it. It was so hot flies weren't even flying.

"Want to shoot a round of pool?" Daddy asked, as we started up Main Street.

"Sure do," I said.

But when we reached the pool room, where ceiling fans sluggishly moved warm air and the players had their sleeves rolled up, it was packed. Saturday wasn't a good day to play pool in La Grange.

"I guess we'd better head back to your grandmother's," Daddy said, slipping me the nickel that two games of pool would have cost.

"I guess so," I said grudgingly. "Thanks for the nickel. But couldn't we wait for a table?"

"We'll play some other time, Joe. It's almost dinner-time."

Heading back up Main Street, we heard raucous laughter. The closer we got to the Courthouse Square, the louder it became. We soon saw the source of the commotion. Near the steps to the courthouse, closed on Saturdays, the rednecks we'd seen in the drugstore were throwing lighted matches and cigarettes at Buttons. Buttons was so hard up for a smoke that he was doing a jig for the whites, trying to catch the lighted cigarettes thrown at him.

"Does the nigger really want a smoke?" the leader of the farmhands asked.

"Yah sir."

"Then take this." The redneck lit a Camel, waved it in the air. "Hold out your hand, nigger."

Buttons complied, and as he did so, the redneck ground the lighted cigarette into the palm of the black man's outstretched hand. Buttons' shrieks filled our ears as he fled.

His misery elicited belly laughter from the whites. "Dumb chocolate drop!" one of them shouted after Buttons.

My daddy had seen enough. "Hey, you!" he shouted to the assailant. "Why don't you try that on me?"

"I'd rather knock your block off, wise guy."

The redneck threw the first punch, but that was the only one he got off. One, two—my daddy's hard right to the jaw and sharp uppercut—sent the bully reeling to the ground. Dumbly, he looked up at my father.

"You should know something, my friend. That man you were picking on served our country in the Great War. He's a war hero. I'd make you lick his boots if he was here."

I already respected my daddy. After that display of Kentucky justice, I idolized him.

The Two Faces of Love

There were other girls before Jo Anne. There was Alice, whose pigtail I loved to pull in the first grade. There was Katherine, who was tall and willowy and got straight A's in the fourth grade and gave me comic Valentines. There was Linda, whose phone number I memorized but never had the courage to call. There was Henrietta, who wandered off with me up a trail in Iroquois Park while we were on a school outing. Sweet Henrietta, whom I longed to kiss. But they were just wisps or desires or unfulfilled fantasies— those other girls. Jo Anne, who came from the mountains, with raven-black hair and green eyes the color of a hidden mountain lake, was real. She was my first love.

Jo Anne came to Louisville in the summer of 1943 with her sister, Sue, to visit her mother, a registered nurse who'd moved to the city to make more money. During the rest of the year, the sisters lived with their grandmother in Blackey, Kentucky.

Until the girls' arrival, my friend Kenny and I had spent the early days of summer in our usual pursuits. We raced our bikes, we explored the neighborhood alleys, and we tested our homemade parachutes from the highest garages we could find. We snuck into Old Man Gallagher's back-yard, where bright orange goldfish swam in a rock-lined pond, and fed them bits of bread. Kenny could run faster than I and could stand on the bars of his bike as it rolled along, a feat I never mastered. He could do just about everything better than I.

It was Kenny who first spotted the sisters as we wheeled up Caldwell Street on our bikes.

"Wow, did you see that?" he shouted back to me after we'd passed the girls, sitting on the front steps of the Caldwell Arms.

"She looked like a tomboy to me," I said.

"I don't mean the one in pigtails, stupid. I mean the one with black hair and the neat tan and the long legs."

Never the shy one, Kenny approached the girls as I trailed behind. From the phonograph in a ground-floor apartment floated the notes of "Don't Sit Under the Apple Tree with Anyone Else But Me," a popular song of the day.

"Sure is a scorcher, isn't it?" Kenny said. "I bet you girls would enjoy an icy cherry Coke."

Jo Anne averted her face. "No, thanks."

Sue was all for it. "I'm thirsty, sis."

Jo Anne snapped: "I don't like to be picked up."

"We're not trying to be fresh," Kenny said in his smoothest manner. "We're just being friendly. After all, you're new to the neighborhood, aren't you?"

"We're visiting my mother," Jo Anne said, "if it's any of your business. She's a registered nurse at Jewish Hospital."

"What a coincidence," Kenny said. "My uncle works there." Kenny was as slick as a sardine. He didn't mention that his uncle was on the Jewish Hospital custodial staff. Soon, he'd won the confidence of both girls, and off we strolled toward Davis Drugstore's soda fountain. Kenny fell in beside Jo Anne and tried to take her hand, but she refused. I ended up with Sue, the two of us not saying a word all the way to the drugstore while Kenny popped off and Jo Anne answered his questions, but nothing more.

While we were sipping our cherry Cokes at the soda fountain, I happened to look into the mirror behind the counter, and my eyes met Jo Anne's. A feeling unlike any other I'd ever felt swept through me. My soul sang. My body tingled. I felt as light as a butterfly. I wanted only one thing: to be alone with her. She looked so intensely and so sweetly into my eyes that I just knew she was feeling something equally monumental. I was so elated I couldn't finish my cherry Coke.

As we were walking back to their building, Kenny asked Jo Anne to go to the movies the next day. She turned him down. My hopes grew.

After we said our good nights, I went home and only picked at my supper. When I went to bed, I couldn't sleep. My head danced with images of Jo Anne. I had the worst kind of love fever. The next day I skipped breakfast and took off early on my bike. I kept circling the apartment building where Jo Anne was staying. I had to see her again.

At last, deliverance came when late in the morning she emerged from the building, alone. She was wearing a sundress and sandals, and her black hair glistened. My heart was thumping so loud I knew she could hear it, too, as I parked my bike and started toward her.

"Where's your sister?" I asked.

"She's gone shopping downtown with my mother. They love to shop."

"Why didn't you go?"

She blushed. "Oh, I guess I thought I might see you again."

"Really?"

From that moment forth, Jo Anne and I were practically inseparable. We liked the same foods, mainly grilled cheese sandwiches and hot dogs and orange Kool-Aid. We went roller-skating, we saw movies, and we had a wiener and marshmallow roast in the backyard of her apartment building. We took a streetcar to Fontaine Ferry Park, where we rode the roller coaster and the Ferris wheel and laughed at the distorted images of ourselves in the curved mirrors of the Funhouse. On our third date, I kissed her squarely on the mouth. After a few weeks I grew bolder, touching her breasts, but that angered her, and I never did it again.

Kenny got mad at me. As far as he was concerned, Jo Anne was *his* girl, although she didn't see it quite that way.

"I saw her first," he'd snap.

"But she likes me," I'd say.

This exact dialogue was repeated between us at least a dozen times. Finally, he stopped dropping by my house and quit speaking to me. I was hurt, but I was ready to give up anything or anyone for Jo Anne.

In August, Jo Anne and Sue took a Greyhound bus back to Blackey. I accompanied them to the station and waved goodbye. Jo Anne was seated nearest the window. She smiled and blew me a kiss. When the bus disappeared around the side of the depot, I felt lost. I moped for days.

For a while, I got letters from her. She was full of plans for *next* summer. Then the letters stopped.

The Louisville winter was severe that year—lots of snow and gloom. I pined for just a note from her. Finally, in the spring, the Dearest Joe letter came. She had met an older guy. She was sorry.

I was heartbroken. I sulked for days, snapped at my mother, picked fights at school.

Later, I realized I'd seen the two faces of love: the fiery, consuming one that takes away all common sense and lifts you into the clouds, and the other face, which, when it dies, leaves a hole in your heart deeper and darker than any other.

The Death Sentence

After the x-ray examination the doctor, a ruby-faced man, asked me to run in place for a minute. Then he listened to my heart. He moved the cold disc of the stethoscope all over my chest and then my back. I could hear his stomach rumbling. When he finished, he told me to put my undershirt and shirt back on and to wait in the adjoining room while he conferred with my mother.

Through the wall I could hear the doctor's booming voice and my mother's almost inaudible responses. What I heard paralyzed me with fear. First, there was to be an operation. Then, I was to be confined to bed for at least a year. He doubted that I'd live beyond my thirtieth birthday.

I began to cry, but I dried my tears before Mother came for me. Gently, she told me I was to have my tonsils removed. My bad cold had turned into strep throat that had, in turn, infected my tonsils, she explained. My heart had been weakened by the infection, she said, sparing me the doctor's full verdict. But I knew I had the same kind of damaged heart that had killed Perry Wilson, my little orphan friend.

I would never be the same after this. My sunny disposition vanished. My love of the outdoors disappeared. I became a kind of hothouse plant, finicky and fragile and fractious.

Because I thought I was dying, I made imperious demands of my mother and father. And these were met. They didn't know I shared the dark secret they so bravely and cheerfully kept from me.

By this time, my father was making a small fortune in business. He had eight employees. He bought foodstuffs by the truck and even freight-load.

It was wartime. Everybody was spending money, and Daddy was coining it.

We now lived in a fourteen-room brick house with marble mantels and a winding staircase. My sick bed, like a prince's throne, dominated the parlor. The room was sunny, with a high ceiling and red brocade wallpaper that gave the room a rosy glow. My bed, moved downstairs from my second-floor bedroom, occupied the space where a sofa and side chairs had stood.

Opposite my bed sat a curio cabinet with its own interior lighting. To please me, my mother bought ceramic dogs and cats and elephants, which she arranged in the cabinet at my direction. Later I developed a penchant for replicas of Egyptian scarabs, and these were also put on display in the cabinet. A bookshelf beside my bed held my novels, my dictionary and a set of Colliers encyclopedias. My typewriter sat on a table with rollers, so that it could be moved to my bedside.

In the parlor it was easy for my mother and our maid, Mattie, an old-fashioned black who wore a red bandanna on her head, to wait on me. And wait on me they did! From the kitchen came tray after tray of cold ginger ale, light soups, snacks and main meals, with desserts galore—silver cups of vanilla and strawberry ice cream, chilled tapioca and chocolate puddings. I kept Mattie busy running to the drugstore for comic books or paperback mystery novels. When she wasn't there, I made the part-time gardener, Oliver, wait on me. Oliver was a black man with a bald head as shiny as a pool ball. Much older than Mattie, he wore white shirts buttoned to the collar and yellow galluses.

On hot afternoons in the summer, Mattie sat patiently by my bed and cooled me with a huge, palm-shaped fan. I had an electric fan, but she thought its breeze was unwholesome, like the night air. "I love to fan my boy," she'd say. She also thought it was bad luck to have flowers in a bedroom. Once my mother heard of Mattie's superstition, she had Oliver remove even the new artificial roses she'd put in a vase on the mantel. Grown more high-strung through the years, Mother believed Mattie's every utterance, as if she were some black voodoo goddess sent to us in our hour of tragedy to deliver us.

I don't think Mattie liked it much when Mother hired my tutor, a middle-aged lady with auburn hair. From her, I learned algebra and Latin. On my own I learned to type. Every day after our lessons, my mother gave the tutor something to take home—a pie, an African violet, a magazine. She took great care to flatter and spoil the tutor, just as she had Mattie, to be sure she kept her under her control.

I became an introspective child, entering forever a land of fantasy. Books. I loved only books now. My favorites were mysteries—Ellery Queen, Erle Stanley Gardner, Dashiell Hammett and S. S. Van Dine. But I also loved Dickens and Thackeray. Oblivious to the changing seasons, I read novels by the stack. I completely turned my back on sports—which I'd once loved—and I guess this was understandable, since I thought I'd never be able to run again.

My day started late, past nine, when Mattie or my mother served breakfast—usually a poached egg, grapefruit or peaches, a dab of grits, hot spiced tea and chilled orange juice. After breakfast I read or worked on my coin or stamp collection. If I became bored, I rang my silver bell, and Mattie would peep her huge, gray-black face into the room. "What you want, chil'?" she'd ask. "I want you to tell me a story," I'd answer.

She was full of them, and she enjoyed telling them, the

two gold teeth in her mouth flashing as she talked. She'd once thrown carbolic acid in a black man's face when he'd tried to rape her. The incident, which had happened thirty years before, stayed fresh in her memory. "Ah see'd that nigger's eyes git big when I throwed the acid at him. He cried out like a hurt dog and run off. He didn't bother me no more. No sir."

After lunch the tutor came. I gave her my homework from the day before, and she went over it with me. She usually left about three o'clock. From then until five or so I studied. Sometimes in the late afternoon Kenny would visit. He'd dropped out of school and was a grocery delivery boy. Already he dated girls, smoked cigarettes and drove an automobile. He was big for his age.

Often I turned on the radio and listened to music or to "Jack Armstrong, The All-American Boy" until Daddy came home, a little after six. This was always an event because he never forgot to bring me something—a box of chocolate-covered cherries or some dates or a yo-yo. Sometimes he'd bring a toy for my dog, a huge, faun-colored Great Dane named Duchess. Or he'd bring me a fountain pen or a new ribbon for my typewriter.

Around seven we ate dinner, my mother and father in the dining room, which adjoined my room, and I in bed. Their table was near the open sliding doors between the rooms, so it was almost as if I sat with them. The three of us talked as we dined, just as if we were at the same table.

If Kenny or my cousin Mae stopped by, we played Tonk at the foot of my bed. Mae, who worked as cashier at a furniture store in downtown Louisville, lived in Crestwood, but she sometimes spent the night with us. I loved to see her coming because she'd bribe me with a dime not to chew gum while she was there. Also, she'd ask me to play "her" song on the piano—"Sentimental Journey" —which also happened to be my mother's favorite tune.

I grew to accept my strange life. The days when I smoked Indian cigars and rode a bike and parachuted off garages and cut school seemed distant to me. The life Kenny led seemed unreal—so adult and far-removed from my own pampered existence.

I wasn't supposed to climb any steps, but on those rare occasions when the house was empty, I explored the upper floors. I remember once or twice going to my old bedroom and playing a Sousa tune on my trumpet. Once I stole one of Daddy's Camels and smoked it. Sometimes I curled up on the front-room window seat and watched the people and traffic below, near yet distant.

I realized I would never be the archeologist I'd always envisioned myself, exploring the heart of Africa and the tombs of the pharaohs and the mysteries of hidden Incan cities. Fate had chosen a different path for me. I would be a writer.

Our maid Mattie fanned me and told me interesting tales when I was confined to bed for a year.

Joe's Place

Joe's, a steamy place with a yellow-brick front and a tangerine awning, was where Male High School's Brahmans—the literary club boys—ate lunch. Tuna fish and egg salad sandwiches and small cartons of sweet or chocolate milk or orange drink were the fare. The pledges of the literary clubs provided the entertainment, pushing pennies across the floor with their noses or doing imitations of teachers. Members of the Hi-Y clubs, considered inferior, ate at the other two restaurants that faced Male High. Only the grinds ate in the school cafeteria.

Willis Price was the crown prince of Joe's Place, and I was one of his loyal followers. He blew a smoke ring so elegantly that other boys would stop eating to watch him. He spoke with a natural whine. His clothes were impeccable, his shoes polished to a gleam, even his shoelaces straight. His family was ancient money. They summered in Europe and spent their Christmases in Florida.

Because my father gave me an automobile when I was fifteen, and I drove it to school when I turned sixteen—one of only three boys in the entire school with an auto—I soon became very popular. This popularity resulted in my being pledged to an elite club and enjoying the privilege of eating at Joe's and moving in the company of Male High's young

Brahmans. Club membership also meant engraved invitations to winter dances. The boys wore tuxes (I had three kinds), and the girls wore evening dresses adorned with orchids. The hotel ballrooms, where the dances were held, all had exotic names: The Rainbow Room, The Flag Room, and The Terrace Room. Music was provided by large bands that ordinarily performed at adult functions.

The first dance I went to was in the Crystal Ballroom at the Brown Hotel. I went stag with some other club members. The room made my senses reel. Cake-shaped chandeliers, with a thousand crystal tears, rained sparkles on the swirling dancers below. In the mirrored walls that enclosed the room, the images of the swirling dancers—the boys in black and the girls in apricot and mint green and daffodil yellow—were an impressionistic blur.

The girls fascinated me. They were so beautiful they seemed unreal. Their perfume intoxicated me. I had taken ballroom-dancing lessons and could dance quite well, but I only watched them. I was too shy to approach them.

A buddy solved my problem by introducing me to bottled courage. He always adhesive-taped a half-pint of whiskey to his leg. During breaks, he'd take a snort in the restroom. I soon started taking my own supply of liquor. With a few drinks under my cummerbund, I lost my shyness. My feet grew nimble, and my tongue loosened. I'd cut in on a guy with a beautiful date and then swirl her about the ballroom until she was breathless. It intoxicated me to see our images spinning past in the mirrors as the band played "Stardust" or "Autumn Nocturne."

Before long I was dating regularly, and a whole new world opened to me. I never knew girls were so soft! I never knew they had problems, too. I didn't know they had headaches and "periods."

In my new and busy life—classwork and dates and club dances and picnics and meetings and R.O.T.C.—I forgot I'd

Striding alongside Joe's Place.

ever been sick. I forgot about dying. I certainly didn't worry about my heart. In fact, the first annual inspection of my R.O.T.C. unit convinced me that, if anything, I had more stamina than most boys.

The inspection came in late spring, and the day was hot. We all were in uniform—hot, heavy, scratchy wool uniforms—and marched a mile to Shelby Park while the Male High Marching Band played the brassy notes of "Under the Double Eagle" and "Stars and Stripes Forever," music that made me lift my head and feel alive. At the park, we stood stiffly at attention for more than an hour as the inspection by regular Army officers from Fort Knox proceeded. Four boys in my company fainted. When the inspection was over, I drank two ice-cold Cokes straight down.

The summer before my senior year, I'd drive my '41 Buick convertible—pearl gray, with red leather seats—to the dances at Big Spring Country Club. The night skies were black velvet and the air aromatic, an amalgam of honeysuckle and sweet rain and the perfume of girls' hair. On these balmy nights, we danced under the stars, the glow of Japanese lanterns brushing our faces. The music of "Deep Purple" swam into our souls. On breaks, we rested on white iron benches under magnolias with enormous creamy blossoms that seemed to glow in the dark.

I met Babs at one of these summer dances. She made my palms sweat, and I couldn't sleep right anymore. I couldn't even dance well with her, and she didn't like boys who drank, so I couldn't use my recently discovered cure-all to help me out. I just had to suffer. I was even jealous when her phone line was busy.

I wrote poetry about her. I didn't show any of it to her because I thought she'd think I was a creep. She was very realistic despite her dreamy appearance.

That summer, she worked as a playground supervisor and art instructor, teaching kids to model clay and paint with watercolors and create mobiles. I'd pick her up every afternoon in the '41 Buick—with the top down; I kept the car shiny and waxed now. I'd take her home, and we'd drink lemonade on her front porch. We continued to date when school started. I took her to football games. All seemed perfect.

Halfway through my senior year, my daddy nearly lost his business. That meant I couldn't go to Princeton. I was crushed. To make matters worse, Babs told me there could never be anything serious between us. I was too young for her, she said. In a blow-up, I told her she'd be sorry. Some day I'd be a U.S. senator or a famous writer, and she'd be sorry she hadn't stuck with me.

I had never even kissed her.

The day of my commencement was the saddest day in my life. We marched in single file into the auditorium while the band played "Pomp and Circumstance." Ahead, already seated on the stage, I saw the smiling faces of many of my classmates. Willis Price, Crown Prince of the Brahmans, was headed to Harvard. Yale had accepted Mike Davis, a friend Babs and I had double-dated with. My Latin class buddy, Tilden McMasters, the class salutatorian, was going to Kenyon.

I had signed up for summer classes at the University of Louisville. My childhood was over.

Louisville Male High School Circa 1949 Brook &
Breckinridge —Louisville, Kentucky

Kenny Mayes (left) and I on a double date at the Club
Madrid, where famous dance bands performed in the
1940s.

An Ode and Thanks

It's no wonder I'm tired. I've produced an estimated six million words, including rough drafts, revisions, throwaways and final copy, in a writing career that's spanned nearly six decades. More than 2,150,000 of these words have been published.

My literary output encompasses 14 published novels (all out of print), nine unpublished novels, numerous short stories, three plays, two screenplays, a children's book, a monograph on the life and films of David Wark Griffith and an unpublished juvenile biography of D.W.G., more than 300 articles in national magazines and another 100 or so in local or regional magazines, play and book reviews plus thousands of newspaper articles, including interviews with Presidents Harry S. Truman, Richard M. Nixon and John F. Kennedy.

My only regret is that two of my best works, a long novel titled *The Thoroughbreds* and a shorter one called *Jacob and His Friends,* have not been published. Is anyone out there listening?

I've survived a devastating tornado, threats on my life when I was an investigative reporter, bar-room brawls, two divorces, alcoholism, a strong addiction to cigarettes (three packs a day), colon cancer, bladder cancer, a heart attack and subsequent quintuple bypass, and a nearly fatal car accident.

Through it all, writing has sustained me. It has been my rock and my refuge. It has chased away my demons. It has given me wings. Without it, I would turn to dust and blow away.

Now a word or two about this memoir. In its original form it is much longer and deals with my entire life. But it is my youth that represents, in historian Thomas Carlyle's words, "the glad season" of my life, and so I have chosen to focus on it.

The sixteen memories I've written about are linked by a common denominator. I'll let you discover what it is.

I extend deep thanks to everyone who helped me research, write, revise, and go to press with this memoir. Especially I thank Mrs. Margaret Russell, the first reader, who highly recommended my work to editors J. T. Lindroos and Kathleen Martin. I also thank my aunt Nancy Grey Oglesby, who so graciously gave me photos and a letter from her D. W. Griffith collection.

I'm equally indebted to my cousin Paula Oglesby Baker for digging up my grandmother's recipe for lemon meringue pie; to Gloria Henson, secretary to the superintendent of the Louisville Baptist Orphans Home, for providing priceless photos that appear in "The Tin Boy"; and to author and old friend Mike Davis for his advice on preparing text and photos for publication via disk.

For their support of several of my literary projects including the production costs of my play "The Dodge", I owe a huge debt of gratitude to David A. and Betty A. Jones. David was a classmate of mine at Male High School, a talented amateur boxer and outstanding student then, chairman of the board of a Fortune 500 company today, a gentleman and a scholar.

Most of all, I thank my wife, Marianna Bachmann Oglesby, for patiently editing my manuscript and for typing numerous drafts and revisions. I also thank my actor-director-writer son, Shane Woodson, for reading the many drafts of my memoir and for suggesting improvements, Spencer and Carol Harper for their friendship and wise counsel for more than 50 years, and Andrew Jefferson Offutt, master of science fiction, my mentor and co-author of my first novel.

Joseph Woodson Oglesby
Louisville, Kentucky
March 9, 2005

www.ingramcontent.com/pod-product-compliance
Lightning Source LLC
Chambersburg PA
CBHW031902090426

42741CB00005B/609